Inside the Spider's Web

by Natalie Lunis

Consultants:

Richard Bradley, PhD
Associate Professor, Emeritus
Evolution, Ecology, and Organismal Biology, The Ohio State University, Columbus, Ohio

Kimberly Brenneman, PhD
National Institute for Early Education Research, Rutgers University, New Brunswick, New Jersey

New York, New York

Credits

Cover, © flySnow/iStockphoto; 3, © iStockphoto/Thinkstock; 4–5, © wittedc/iStockphoto; 6, © Dave Pressland/FLPA; 7, © Photo Fun/Shutterstock; 8B, © Stephen Dalton/Photoshot; 10, © Konrad Wothe/Minden Pictures/FLPA; 11, © Fabio Liverani/Naturepl; 12, © Kian-Peng Sim; 13, © Roger Dauriac/Biosphoto/FLPA; 14, © Paul S. Wolf/Shutterstock; 15, © Nick Upton/Naturepl; 16, © Ron O'Connor/Naturepl; 17, © Kelly Nelson/Shutterstock; 18–19, © Malcolm Schuyl/FLPA; 20, © Jason Swain; 21, © Konrad Wothe/Minden Pictures/FLPA; 23TL, © Paul S. Wolf/Shutterstock; 23TC, © Kelly Nelson/Shutterstock; 23TR, © Kian-Peng Sim; 23BL, © Smit/Shutterstock; 23BC, © Nick Upton/Naturepl; 23BR, © Fabio Liverani/Naturepl; 24, © iStockphoto/Thinkstock.

Publisher: Kenn Goin
Editorial Director: Adam Siegel
Creative Director: Spencer Brinker
Design: Emma Randall
Photo Researcher: Ruby Tuesday Books Ltd

Library of Congress Cataloging-in-Publication Data

Lunis, Natalie.
  Inside the spider's web / by Natalie Lunis.
      pages cm. — (Snug as a bug: where bugs live)
  Includes bibliographical references and index.
  ISBN-13: 978-1-61772-903-4 (library binding)
  ISBN-10: 1-61772-903-5 (library binding)
  1. Orb weavers—Juvenile literature. I. Title.
  QL458.42.A7L86 2014
  595.4'4—dc23
                        2013002677

For more information, write to Bearport Publishing Company, Inc., 45 West 21st Street, Suite 3B, New York, New York 10010. Printed in the United States of America.

10 9 8 7 6 5 4 3 2 1

Contents

Welcome to the Web

On a summer day, the sun rises over a grassy yard.

Tiny drops of water catch the sun's light.

Some of them outline a shape that looks like a bicycle wheel.

A little creature sits in the center of the wheel.

It is a spider waiting in its web.

spider

spiderweb

A spiderweb that is shaped like a wheel is called an orb web. *Orb* means "circle."

Meet the Orb Weavers

There are about 43,000 different kinds of spiders.

About 4,600 kinds weave wheel-shaped webs that are known as orb webs.

Scientists have given these spiders names that tell where they make their webs.

For example, barn spiders often make their orb webs in and around barns.

Garden spiders make their webs in gardens, yards, and fields.

a garden spider's orb web

What do you think spiders use to make their webs? Where do they get this material?

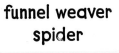

funnel weaver
spider

funnel weaver
spiderweb

Not all
web-weaving
spiders make webs
that look like orbs. Some
make webs that look
like loose tangles,
funnels, sheets,
or tubes.

Making the Web

A spider makes its web out of silky threads that come out of the back of its body.

To begin its web, a spider lets out one thread.

The thread drifts in the air until it sticks to a spot, such as a twig.

The spider builds the rest of its web around this silky strand.

A spider's silk starts out as a liquid. However, it dries and becomes thread-like as the spider pulls it out with its feet.

1 A spider begins its web with one silk thread.

silk thread

silk thread

spider's feet

2 The spider crawls across the thread, adding stronger silk.

3 Then it adds a set of straight lines that meet in the web's center.

4 Next, the spider lets out silk as it moves in a spiral path.

5 Finally, the spider eats up the spiral path and replaces it with silk that is sticky.

What do you think the sticky silk in the spiral part of the web is for?

9

A Deadly Trap

After making its web, a spider waits on the silky threads.

The sticky parts of the web help the spider catch its food.

Flies, crickets, moths, and other **insects** hit the web as they fly or jump through the air.

Sometimes, they can escape right away.

Other times, their bodies stick to the gluey silk.

a moth stuck in a web

mayflies

Why doesn't a spider get stuck in its own web? It knows which parts are not sticky and walks only on them.

How do you think a spider knows when an insect is caught in its web?

11

Dinnertime!

When a spider feels its web shaking, it runs over to the trapped insect.

Then the spider grabs its victim and wraps it up with silk.

The spider might kill and eat the insect right away or save it for later.

fangs

A spider kills its **prey** by biting it with two **fangs** that send a deadly poison into the victim's body.

grasshopper

a spider wrapping
its prey in silk

Dropping to Safety

Orb-weaving spiders set dangerous traps for flies and other insects.

Yet the eight-legged creatures have enemies of their own.

To escape from birds and other **predators**, a spider often makes a **dragline**.

It attaches one end of a long silk thread to a branch near its web.

Then it quickly drops out of sight until the danger is gone.

dragline

Many kinds of birds, frogs, lizards, and wasps eat orb-weaving spiders.

spider

wasp

Besides getting away from an enemy, why else might a spider leave its web?

15

Meeting and Mating

In the fall, male spiders leave their webs.

They go off to find females so that they can mate and have babies.

After mating, a female orb weaver makes a silk **egg sac**.

Then she lays hundreds of eggs inside it.

She attaches the sac to her web or to another safe place.

male spider

female spider

Like other kinds of female spiders, female orb weavers sometimes attack and eat the much smaller males that come to their webs. Most of the time, however, they mate with their male visitors.

female spider

egg sac

Inside the Egg Sac

An egg sac keeps a spider's eggs safe and dry during winter.

Then, in spring, the eggs hatch.

Hundreds of baby spiders—called spiderlings—chew through the egg sac and start crawling around.

The spiderlings are tiny at first, but they grow fast.

Orb-weaving spiders live for less than a year. Males die shortly after mating. Females die soon after laying their eggs.

spiderlings

Look at the spiderlings and compare them to adult spiders. How are they like the adults? How are they different?

Up, Up, and Away!

After leaving its egg sac, a spiderling needs to find a place to live.

It climbs to a high place, such as the top of a plant.

Then the tiny spider lets out a strand of silk and waits for a breeze to carry it away.

When the spider lands, it finds a spot where insects are sure to pass by.

Once there, it starts to weave its first web!

spiderling

silk strand

Orb webs are strong, but they can tear in the wind or when insects get caught in them. The silk also loses its stickiness as the web dries. As a result, an orb-weaving spider usually needs to make a new web each day.

Science Lab

Make a Model

Imagine that you are a scientist who is teaching people about orb-weaving spiders and their webs.

Make a model that will help people understand how the web is made and how it helps the spider survive.

You will need:

- A small ball of yarn
- A piece of cardboard about the size of this book
- White glue

1. Cut the yarn into six pieces that are each six inches (15 cm) long. Make one piece that is about two feet (.6 m) long.

2. Use the glue to make the web's straight lines on the cardboard. Use this picture as a guide.

3. Place the six-inch (15 cm) pieces of yarn on top of the glue.

4. Use the glue to make the web's spiral. Use this picture as a guide.

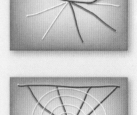

5. Place the long piece of yarn on top of the glue.

When you are finished, present your model to friends and family members.

Science Words

dragline (DRAG-line) a silk thread that a spider can use to drop down from a high place

egg sac (EG SAK) the silk container that a female spider makes to hold and protect her eggs

fangs (FANGZ) hard, pointed mouthparts used to send poison into prey

insects (IN-sekts) small animals that have six legs, three main body parts, two antennas, and a hard covering called an exoskeleton

predators (PRED-uh-turs) animals that hunt and eat other animals

prey (PRAY) animals that are hunted and caught for food by other animals

Index

Read More

Berger, Melvin. *Spinning Spiders.* New York: HarperCollins (2003).

Bishop, Nic. *Spiders.* New York: Scholastic (2007).

White, Nancy. *Crafty Garden Spiders (No Backbone! The World of Invertebrates).* New York: Bearport (2009).

Learn More Online

To learn more about spiders and their webs, visit **www.bearportpublishing.com/SnugasaBug**

About the Author

Natalie Lunis has written many science and nature books for children, including books about black widow spiders and desert tarantulas. She lives in the Hudson River Valley, just north of New York City.